# Reality TV

## by Adam Woog

ERICKSON PRESS

Yankton, South Dakota

# ERICKSON PRESS

Library of Congress Control Number: 2007920461
ISBN-13: 978-1-60217-005-6

Printed in the United States of America

# Contents

# Reality TV Invades Earth's Airwaves!

On May 24, 2006, a silver-haired singer from Alabama was voted "the best unknown performer in America." This was Taylor Hicks. Taylor's success ended season five of America's most popular TV show, *American Idol*.

About 36 million people watched that show. Over 63 million votes were sent in. That is a lot of people and votes. During *American Idol's* regular season, millions of people watch new episodes every week!

And *American Idol* is just one show. There are hundreds of reality shows all over the world. New ones are invented all the time. In fact, so many exist that not even experts can guess how many there are.

Reality TV has invaded Earth—and people love it. Tens of millions of fans watch their favorite shows every night of the week. They want to know who will get ahead in *The Amazing Race*. Or who will get kicked off *Survivor*. Or who will get fired on *The Apprentice*.

# Part of Daily Life

Fans of reality TV like it because it is fun. But reality shows are more than just an evening's fun. They have become part of everyday life.

People like to talk about their favorite shows at school or work. They like finding news and gossip about stars and shows through TV, magazines, newspapers, and the Internet. And a really exciting event, like Taylor Hicks winning on *American Idol,* is front-page news.

People who *watch* reality shows often hope to *be* on them, too. So when a show has auditions in a city, thousands of hopeful stars appear. If they

Taylor Hicks was *American Idol'*s big winner in May 2006.

A contestant on *The Amazing Race* glides over a steep canyon in South America.

have to, they will even camp out all night to get a chance. Newspaper reporter Pam Sitt comments, "Apparently, there is no sleep for those chasing a dream."[1]

# Here to Stay

Reality TV is not new. It has been around for many years. However, it did not become really popular until the late 1990s. Now it is so popular, it may be here to stay.

Many experts think that reality shows will remain on TV, just like sitcoms, talk shows, sports, and dramas. Already, the Emmy Awards show has created two honors for reality shows.

So just what is this thing that has taken over TV?

# Chapter 1

# What Is Reality TV?

Reality TV can make us laugh. It can gross us out. It can confuse us. It can even teach us something. It is also based on real life. In a way, reality TV is *like* real life, but with a few big differences.

For one thing, reality TV is not random the way real life is. A show's producers choose its cast, locations, and events. This way, the producers can make sure the show is as exciting and interesting as possible.

Producers can also decide, in other ways, how close a show is to real life. For example, they can edit film to change a story line. Or they can ask participants to act in certain ways to make things more interesting.

Reality TV is not like real life in one other big way. In real life, video cameras usually do not record everything we do!

Reality TV, then, is not exactly like real life. But it pretends to be, at least most of the time. And that is one reason why viewers like it so much. Reality TV *feels* real.

Reality TV uses real life as its base. So almost anything can give producers an idea for a show. This means that many different kinds of shows are part of reality TV.

## Competition Shows

The most popular kind of reality show is the competition show. In competition shows, people try to outdo each other in contests. Winners can end up with a date, a spouse, lots of money, a good job, or even worldwide fame.

Teenagers are huge fans of reality TV shows.

# A Brief History of Reality TV

Reality TV shows are not new. The first was *Candid Camera* in 1948, at the beginning of the TV age. It played pranks on people and recorded what happened. In 1950 came shows like *Beat the Clock* and *Truth or Consequences*, which had crazy competitions and practical jokes. Another important show was the PBS series *An American Family* in 1973. It showed the breakup of a real family.

But reality TV really took off after the start of *COPS* in 1989. It was very popular, and its shaky camera style influenced much of future reality TV. Soon after, a writer's strike forced producers to create shows that did not need written scripts. Presto, the Age of Reality TV was born!

Allen Funt (right) created and hosted *Candid Camera,* the first reality TV show.

Competition shows like *Survivor* have huge followings.

The top competition show in the United States is *American Idol. Survivor* is also very popular. *Survivor* strands a group of people in a remote place, such as a tropical island or a desert. The group is divided into "tribes."

The tribes have to survive with only a few resources. The tribes also compete against each other. When a tribe loses, it votes a member out. As the tribes shrink, they join together. They keep voting people out until only one is left.

Another competition show is *The Apprentice.* On this show, teams of people work together. The one who does the best gets a good job and high pay for one year. But those who do poorly are kicked off the show. The show's host, real estate tycoon Donald Trump, tells them, "You're fired!"

# Underdogs

Competition shows are popular for many reasons. People like the drama created by players battling against each other. It is exciting to watch players get ahead or fall behind. And people also enjoy watching people in power throw their weight around. An example of this is Simon Cowell, the mean judge on *American Idol.*

Many people also like to root for an underdog —that is, someone who does not seem to have much chance of winning. One example of an underdog who came out on top was William Hung. He was on the third season of *American Idol.* Hung had no talent for singing or dancing, but he was eager and good-natured. Viewers reacted to his good attitude by making him a surprise star.

# Makeover Shows

Another popular type of reality show is the makeover show, on which something is changed. For example, on *Trading Spaces,* two families redecorate rooms in each other's homes. On *Pimp My Ride* and *Trick My Truck,* cars or trucks in bad shape are turned into dream rides.

American Idol judges are almost as popular with TV watchers as the contestants.

## Real People Watching Real People

**Many people have pointed out that, on reality TV, viewers can watch people who are just like them or who are completely different. Nely Galan, creator of *The Swan*, comments,**

> **Human beings ultimately want to watch themselves, and reality TV has really shown people that reality is stranger than fiction. Ultimately, the stars of reality TV are real people. I find it fascinating, because we spend so many years idolizing celebrities, and now real people get a shot at it, and of course they love it.**

Matthew Robinson, *How to Get on Reality TV*. New York: Random House Reference, 2005, p. 85.

Some shows take this idea even further. They let people change themselves. For example, people on *Extreme Makeover* undergo things like plastic surgery and weight loss. They become "new" people.

A less extreme show is *Queer Eye*. On this program, gay fashion experts help people change their habits. These people end up with new styles of clothing, new house decoration, new ways of cooking, and so on.

Makeover shows such as these are popular for many reasons. It is exciting to see someone's looks or home change. Also, the stars of the shows, such as *Queer Eye*'s "Fabulous Five," are fun to watch.

These shows can also inspire viewers to change their own lives. For example, a woman named Suzy Preston lost 95 pounds on a weight-loss show, *The Biggest Loser.*

After she won, some of Suzy's friends decided to lose weight too. One of them, Stephanie Pond, said, "Everybody around me started losing weight

On an episode of *Queer Eye,* Jai Rodriguez coaches Red Sox player Jason Varitek.

because they were inspired by watching Suzy. I was not going to be the last of the fat friends!"[2]

# Flies on the Wall

Another popular type of reality show is the fly-on-the-wall show. These shows allow viewers to follow people as they lead their lives. It is as if viewers were flies on the wall, seeing everything that goes on.

A classic example of this kind of show is *The Real World.* It began in 1992. Each season on this show, a group of strangers meets and shares a house. Cameras film the group throughout the time they spend together. The cameras record how the group's relations to each other grow and change. Sometimes friends are made. Sometimes enemies are made.

Another classic fly-on-the-wall show is *COPS*. It started back in 1989. Its film crews follow police officers as they do their jobs. The cameras record what happens. Viewers see the officers answering calls, making arrests, and so on.

Fly-on-the-wall shows use the everyday lives of people to keep things interesting. But there can also be an added twist. For example, *Texas Ranch House* added a historical spin. For two and a half months, fifteen people lived exactly as if they were on a Texas cattle ranch in 1867. They had to do chores like repairing fences, herding cows, cooking, and cleaning house. But they had to do these without any modern tools!

Evan Marriott (left) never knew what would happen on *Joe Millionaire.*

## Keeping Secrets

The makers of reality shows keep lots of secrets. They even keep secrets from their stars. Evan Marriott starred in *Joe Millionaire.* He did not know what would happen on the show until the last minute. The show was being filmed in France. "The day before I left for France, I signed . . . papers which said what the show was about. At that point, could I really back out?"

Quoted in James Poniewozik, "Why Reality TV Is Good for Us," *Time,* February 17, 2003.

# Watching Celebrities

Some fly-on-the-wall shows use a different twist. They follow famous people around. For example, *The Osbournes* follows the crazy life of rock singer Ozzy Osbourne's family. There is also *The Simple Life*. On this show, rich girls Paris Hilton and Nicole Richie trade their grand lives for common ones, such as living with a plain farm family.

Cameras record the unusual life of Ozzy Osbourne and his family in *The Osbournes*.

People like to watch fly-on-the-wall shows for many reasons. One is that viewers can peek "backstage" at hidden worlds. Viewers can learn about everyday people, such as the police on *COPS*. Or they can find out what life was like in a period of history, as on *Texas Ranch House*. Or they can watch famous people, as on *The Osbournes*.

Fly-on-the-wall shows and other kinds of reality TV are supposed to just follow the events of real life. But shows like *Texas Ranch House* or *The Simple Life* are created on purpose. After all, in real life, people do not usually live as if it were 1867. And in real life, rich people do not usually give up their lives for plain ones.

At least partly, therefore, these shows are not real. So how real is reality TV, anyway?

# Chapter 2

# How Real Is Reality TV?

**T**he producers of a dating show, *The Dating Experiment*, had a problem. One of the women on the show did not like one of the men who wanted to date her. But the producers thought it would be a better and more exciting story if the woman liked him. So they played a trick on the woman. They taped an interview with her. They asked about her favorite movie star. She said, "Whenever I see Adam Sandler, he's so cute, so funny, so handsome that I just want to go up and hug him."[3]

Later, the producers took Sandler's name out of the tape and put something else in instead. They used her voice saying the name of the man she did not like. Now they had tape that "proved" that the woman liked someone she really did not like!

## Frankenbiting

TV producers have a name for this trick. They call it frankenbiting. This word combines

Cutting and frankenbiting are tricks of the reality TV trade.

*Frankenstein*'s monster (who was made out of spare parts) and *sound bite*, which means "a short bit of recorded speech."

According to insiders, TV producers often use such tricks to change the "reality" of shows. TV producers will use many different methods to make sure that their shows are exciting, fast-moving, and interesting. The first, of course, is to choose the right players and locations.

The second is to cleverly edit the show. Every reality show must use editing. There is no way around this. A typical hour-long show (about 42 minutes, minus commercials) has been edited from dozens, even hundreds, of hours of tape.

Without editing, these hundreds of hours of raw tape would put everyone to sleep. Imagine a fly-on-the-wall show like *The Real World* being

One reason people like to watch reality shows is they hope to be on them.

## Cheating

Several people have been kicked off reality shows because they have broken the rules. For example, Gabriel Iglesias was banned in 2006 from *Last Comic Standing* for using a Blackberry and making extra phone calls. (He was only allowed one a day.) Iglesias said that he was simply calling his girlfriend, but a series of "spoiler" leaks about the show's secrets stopped after he left. Many people thought that Iglesias had been secretly feeding news to the outside.

In another case, designer Keith Michael was kicked off *Project Runway* in 2006. His crime was possessing pattern-making books. These were not allowed because they made it unfair for the others. Michael commented, "I'm off the show, and I'm going to be a laughingstock to my friends."

Todd Camp, "When 'Reality' TV Runs up Against the Rules," *Seattle Times*, September 4, 2006, p. E2.

shown 24 hours a day, seven days a week, with no editing and with all of its hidden cameras going at once. Who would watch it?

# "Snapshots of Reality"

Editing raw tape lets a show's producers change its amount of reality. The producers can keep some things and leave others out. It is like seeing snap-shot photographs, says Nick Lachey. Nick costarred with his wife, Jessica Simpson, on a reality show, *Newlyweds*. (They are not married any more.) He says, "I wouldn't really say it was completely real. I'd describe the show as being a series of snapshots of reality—which, you have to remember, was edited all for your entertainment pleasure!"[4]

The changes made by editing vary a lot from show to show. Some shows, even after editing,

Some of the *Newlyweds* show was filmed at the mansion of Jessica Simpson and Nick Lachey.

still give a fairly true picture of what really happened. Others change things a lot. The story line can change. So can what people say and do. Even the way a show ends can be different after editing.

For example, someone who used to edit the show *Blind Date* says that the show's scenes were sometimes put together out of order. This was done to keep it lively. For example, the producers might want to make a man seem bored while on a date. So they showed his date talking, then showed a shot of him looking bored. In fact, these two shots were filmed at different times. Editing just made it seem like they happened at the same time. The man seemed to really be bored.

# Tricks of the Trade

Producers can use many other tricks as well. For example, insiders have said that the producers of the show *Joe Millionaire* put tape from different times together. This created scenes that never really happened. Another example happened on *The Simple Life*, according to insiders. The producers wrote some of Paris Hilton's dialogue, instead of using what she made up as she went along.

Also, if the cameras were not there when an interesting thing happened, producers can make the scene happen again. They do this even though the second time is not "real." For example, someone

# A Taste of Reality, Eighteenth-Century Style

One show that stayed close to reality with little trickery was *The Ship*, on the History Channel in 2002. It followed 40 people, mostly with no experience as sailors. They sailed a replica of the ship of a famous explorer, Captain James Cook. They were able to travel along one of Cook's voyages, from Australia to Indonesia in 1770.

The crew shared some of the same hardships that explorers like Cook had. They had to sleep in hammocks, eat bad diets (mostly oatmeal, salt beef, sauerkraut, dried fish, and hard biscuits), and do back-breaking daily chores.

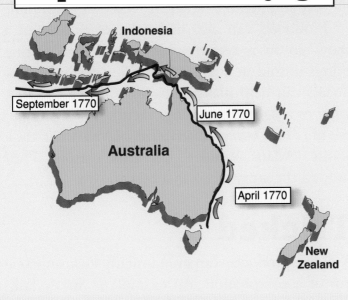

## Captain Cook's Voyage

Indonesia

September 1770

June 1770

Australia

April 1770

New Zealand

Nicole Richie (left) and Paris Hilton starred in *The Simple Life*. Some scenes in the show were not real.

on *The Restaurant* was asked to copy a fall that broke his elbow. The first time, it was a real accident; the second time, the "accident" was caught on film.

Producers can also make the story line on a show go in a certain way, rather than letting things unfold in a natural way. For example, producers can help make sure something like a love affair or a fight keeps things exciting. The producers of *The Dating Experiment* played their trick about "Adam Sandler" for this reason. They wanted the story to go in a certain way.

## Tricked

A show's producers can even unfairly kick someone out of a competition. An example is Stacey Stillman, who was on the first season of *Survivor*. She says that others on the show were forced to vote her off. This was because the producers wanted another person, a 72-year-old man, to stay.

Another way to "change reality," according to insiders, is to hire actors to play ordinary people. For example, some dating shows such as *Blind Date* sometimes use models and actresses to play "real" people. Jeannie Kim, who appeared on *Blind Date*, comments about the show's producers: "They highly stress, 'Do not tell your date you're an actress or model.' They'd rather you say you're a bartender or waitress. I actually had a boyfriend when I went on *Blind Date*. I just went on to promote myself, as do a lot of my girlfriends."[5]

*Survivor* contestants Susan Hawk and 72-year-old Rudy Boesch discuss the reality show.

# Percentage of Youth Who Have Watched These Reality Shows

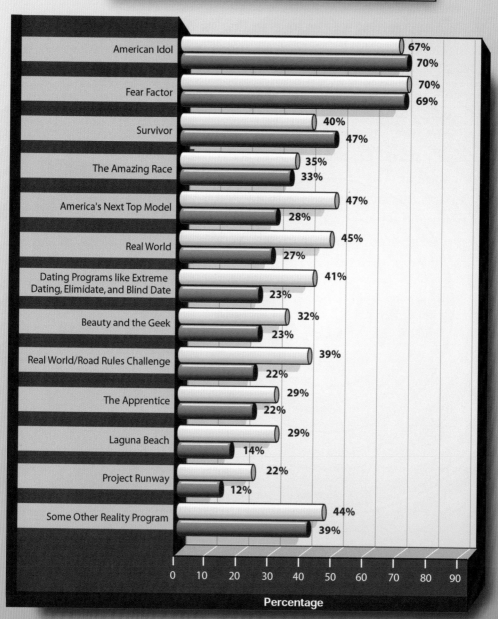

☐ 13–18 year olds    ■ 8–12 year olds

| Show | 13–18 year olds | 8–12 year olds |
|------|-----------------|----------------|
| American Idol | 67% | 70% |
| Fear Factor | 70% | 69% |
| Survivor | 40% | 47% |
| The Amazing Race | 35% | 33% |
| America's Next Top Model | 47% | 28% |
| Real World | 45% | 27% |
| Dating Programs like Extreme Dating, Elimidate, and Blind Date | 41% | 23% |
| Beauty and the Geek | 32% | 23% |
| Real World/Road Rules Challenge | 39% | 22% |
| The Apprentice | 29% | 22% |
| Laguna Beach | 29% | 14% |
| Project Runway | 22% | 12% |
| Some Other Reality Program | 44% | 39% |

Percentage

Source: Harris Interactive YouthQuery℠ online omnibus, March 15 to 20, 2006; n= 1,373 U.S. youth ages 8 to 18.

# Trickery on Purpose

Sometimes the tricks on reality TV are no secret. The viewers know about the tricks. For instance, on *Joe Millionaire,* many women were in competition to connect with a handsome man. The women thought he was a millionaire looking for a wife. But the viewers knew that "Joe" was really a poor construction worker.

Another program that fooled its players was *My Big Fat Obnoxious Boss.* On this show, people did crazy little jobs (such as selling reusable toilet paper) in order to win a real job. The viewers knew there was no job. The whole thing was a hoax.

A twist on this idea was used for *Joe Schmo.* One person on this show thought he was taking part in a reality show called *Lap of Luxury.* What he did not know was that the whole thing was a fake. Everyone else on the show was an actor— and the viewers knew it!

Another show, *Punk'd,* plays elaborate practical jokes on famous people, then catches the fun with hidden cameras. On one show, for example, a basketball star, Allen Iverson, was kept from going to his own birthday party. He was told that he could not go into a club for security reasons. He was told that the president's daughters and their Secret Service men were inside the building. When he learned the truth, Allen did not think it was very funny!

# It's Not True— So What?

Fans of reality TV know that their shows are not "real." This is not news. According to a recent *Time* magazine poll, only 30 percent of reality TV watchers thought that the shows were true pictures of what really happens. And 25 percent believed that reality TV is almost completely made up.

On the other hand, over half the people polled said that this did not change their enjoyment of the programs. To them it did not matter that reality TV is not real.

For these fans it is enough that a show is entertaining. They would rather watch an interesting story that is a little fictional than a boring but totally true one. In other words, it is no big deal if producers change things a little. *Time* magazine's TV critic, James Poniewozik, says, "Cheating? Sure. But viewers want suspense."[6]

So in the end the tricks that producers use may not matter. They certainly do not seem to bother the millions of reality TV fans around the world. They still watch their favorite shows every night. Thanks to them, reality TV rules in almost every corner of the globe.

# Reality TV Goes Global

One of Guatemala's most popular shows is *Desafio 10* ("Challenge 10"). Ten young men who are strangers to each other live together for two weeks. They study subjects such as marketing and customer service. They divide into two groups. Each team starts a small business. One opens a shoeshine and shoe repair shop. The other starts a car wash.

Sounds kind of boring, right? But it is not. Why? All ten men are former members of dangerous gangs. These gangs have been linked to many drug sales and murders. The men used to be rivals! The show's creator, Harold Sibaja, comments that they are the sort of people that "everybody wants dead or in jail."[7]

## Made in the USA

As a result, *Desafio 10* has plenty of excitement. The show was inspired by two American shows, *The Real World* and *The Apprentice*. It is just one

Rap star Xzibit stands in front of a tricked-out car from custom-car show *Pimp My Ride.*

example of how an idea from one country can be changed for viewers in other countries.

*Pimp My Ride* is another show that has been a hit around the world. However, it changes from country to country. For instance, German TV has *Pimp My Fahrrad* ("Pimp My Bicycle") and *Pimp My Whatever.* On this show, a crew of workers redoes just about anything. On one episode, a tiny, broken-down doghouse became a doggie castle complete with red carpeting, a drawbridge, a stereo, and even a Webcam.

# Ideas from Other Places

America has the most reality TV, and many shows started here. But some programs that are big hits in America started in other countries. For example, *Big Brother* started in the Netherlands. *Survivor* started in Sweden as *Expedition Robinson*. *American Idol* was first an English show called *Pop Idol*. And *Trading Spaces* also started in England, where it was called *Changing Rooms*.

## Starting over in Lebanon

Several reality shows that broadcast in Arab countries have been successes. This is sometimes a surprise, since these countries are usually very strict. Shows that focus on women are especially surprising. This is because women often are thought of as second-class citizens.

One of these shows is a show from Lebanon called *Min Jadid* (Starting Over). On it, six women live together in a deluxe apartment in Beirut, the capitol of Lebanon. Mental health workers, fashion experts, and other advisers help the women with their personal problems. These problems range from intense shyness to starting a business. The show is helping to overcome some of the stereotypes about women in Arab countries.

Crazy-stunt shows like *Fear Factor* and *Jackass* were inspired by Japanese game shows. On these shows, people compete for prizes by doing wacky, gross, and sometimes dangerous stunts. A classic was *Takeshi's Castle*.

On *Takeshi's Castle*, an actor played a count in a castle. People had to play crazy games to win control of the castle. For example, for one stunt they dressed up as birds and "flew" down a wire. While moving, they had to grab a rabbit and drop it into a nest so that their "baby birds" could eat. Meanwhile, other people were throwing soccer balls at them. It was difficult!

# Reality Elsewhere

*Takeshi's Castle* was a big hit in the 1980s, and people all over Asia still love reality shows. Asia has its own 24-hour reality TV network and dozens of shows. For instance, a popular show in Indonesia is *Uang Kaget*, "Surprise Money." On this show, people receive about $1,000. But they have to spend it in a short time. They have to return whatever money is left over. The camera follows them as they rush around a store, trying to spend quickly.

Sometimes Asian TV producers travel far to create their shows. For example, the Chinese series *Quest* followed four teams on a road trip from Boston to Miami. Each team was named for the birthplace of its members: Team Hong Kong, Team Taiwan, and Team China (all parts of

The cast of the popular reality show *Jackass* clowns around in London.

Greater China), plus Team U.S.A. All the participants had lived in the United States for many years. As they traveled, they challenged each other at tasks such as gambling in a casino, making wooden barrels, and milking cows.

# Reality TV in Iraq

People in the Middle East also have become reality TV fans. For example, a popular show in Iraq is called *Materials and Labor*. This show was inspired by *Extreme Makeover: Home Edition*. The show follows crews as they fix buildings at no cost to their owners. The twist is that all the buildings have been damaged by bombs and other violence.

In one episode of *Materials and Labor*, workers were shown in Baghdad, the capital of Iraq. They hammered nails, laid bricks, and poured concrete to rebuild a woman's house. A bomb had destroyed it. For the homeowner, watching the workers was thrilling. She said, "I get chills thinking about this. Words can't express how grateful I am."[8]

*Extreme Makeover: Home Edition* has won special awards for being creative.

## Hidden Faces

Team members in *Desafio 10* did not want anyone to know who they were. They wore masks while on camera. Rival gangs could not see their faces. Rival gangs did not know who they were. But after a while most *Desafio 10* members took their masks off. They decided to show their faces. They decided that they did not need to be afraid.

# *Big Brother Africa*

Reality TV also has reached Africa. *Big Brother Africa* is filmed in English. In it, people from many countries live together in a sealed house. They are watched constantly by cameras.

As on the American version, problems arise among the show's members. Then they try to solve these problems. On one episode, they had to learn each other's national anthems. They got angry because they could not agree on who should sing first.

Bayo, from Nigeria, got very mad. He thought that Alex, from Kenya, had insulted him. Bayo walked away, saying that no one ever listened to him. Then Stefan, from Namibia, told Bayo, "Don't behave in this way, because the entire house will suffer."[9]

Sometimes the housemates in *Big Brother Africa* get into fights.

# Solving Problems

That fight was a small thing, but it stood for a big challenge. For decades, Africa has had serious problems like war and poverty. Many people have tried to bring Africa's nations together so that they can work out these problems. So far, there has been little success.

But *Big Brother Africa* has viewers from about 40 countries. Its evidence represents many different cultures. Its producers hope that people on the show will learn to like each other. They further hope that this will be good for viewers. Lorraine Onyango, a student in Kenya and a fan of

## Group TV Watching

*Big Brother Africa* is very popular in Africa. But it is only popular among people who have access to TV. Very few Africans have a TV. Only about 4 percent of people in Africa own a TV. So millions watch *Big Brother Africa* and other shows in groups. In many villages people gather around a TV in a bar or club. In some cases, it is the only TV in the whole village.

Devoted fans enjoy watching scenes like this from *Big Brother Africa*.

The people living as housemates in *Big Brother Africa* go about their daily business.

the program, agrees. She says, "They're learning about each other, and that's interesting."[10]

As shows like *Big Brother Africa* are filmed, most of the people who are in them have a good time. Their lives afterward are often good as well. But sometimes life after reality TV takes a strange turn.

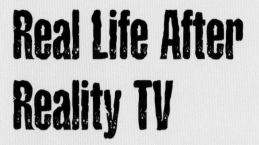

# Real Life After Reality TV

**W**hen William Hung was on *American Idol* in 2004, no one thought he would become a star. Hung was a mild-mannered engineering student from Hong Kong. He was not a real performer. In fact, it was clear that he had almost no talent.

Hung did not impress the *Idol* judges. Simon Cowell made fun of him. Paula Abdul and Randy Jackson tried hard not to laugh. In fact, Jackson had to hide his face so Hung would not see him crack up.

But William kept his spirits up. He did not get angry, as other people did when the judges made fun of them. Instead he said, "I already gave my best, and I have no regrets at all."[11]

## William Hung, Superstar

Abdul told Hung that she liked his spirit. Many of the show's viewers also liked it. Very quickly,

William Hung
became a huge star
after appearing on
*American Idol*.

and against the odds, Hung became world-famous.

He was kicked off *American Idol.* Yet Hung's appearance made him a superstar. He was asked to be on many other TV shows and other live appearances. Web sites were created about him. Magazines and newspapers had stories about him. *Saturday Night Live* even made fun of him. Hung has stayed in the public eye since then. His career includes recordings, commercials, and a halftime performance at a pro basketball game.

Perhaps Hung became a star partly because some people just liked laughing at him. But other people responded to his sincere spirit. One fan said, "He's just very real. He doesn't care whether he's fashionable or not. He has a really good time performing, and he really gives it his all, just for the love of it."[12]

# Good Times, Bad Times

Of course, Hung is not the only person on *Idol* who has become famous. Many others have gone on to good careers. Among them are Clay Aiken, Taylor Hicks, Kelly Clarkson, Fantasia Barrino, and Ruben Studdard.

However, some people who were on reality TV have had bad times during and after the taping of their shows. For them, there was too much stress. They did not like having cameras, other players,

Superstar William
Hung wows the
crowds during
halftime at an
NBA game in 2004.

and producers around all the time. Toni
Johnson-Woods is an Australian professor
and the author of a book on reality TV.
She says, "People are not aware of how
probing [nosy] the eye of the camera can
be. There is definite potential for psycho-
logical [emotional] harm."[13]

Because of the stress, many people have acted strangely while their show was being taped. For instance, on *Big Brother*'s second season, Justin Sebik was kicked off for acting weirdly. His actions included holding a knife to another person's throat.

Another example was on the version of *Big Brother* from Portugal. One contestant, who was a kick-boxing instructor, kicked a housemate in the face. (He was kicked off the show!) Also, on the African version of *Big Brother*, one man began

## The Great Reality TV Swindle

One producer persuaded 30 people to leave their homes and jobs to star in a reality TV show in England. He promised food, clothing, shelter, and a prize of about $150,000. But it was all a fake.

When the contestants arrived in London to begin the show, they were told to form three teams and try to raise about $1.5 million first. They also learned that their food and lodging would not be free.

When they complained, the producer admitted that the whole project was fantasy. The people were furious. They locked him in a house and talked to a real TV producer. This producer made a TV show about the hoax. The people finally got their moment on TV after all. It was just not the way they had planned.

Kelly Clarkson became a famous singer after winning the first-ever *American Idol* contest in 2002.

secretly burying spoons in the garden. And someone on *Big Brother* in England started keeping piles of dead batteries for no reason.

# Trouble

The stress often keeps going after people return to normal life. Sometimes these former players get into trouble, although this is usually minor. For instance, a Connecticut fireman on *Big Brother*, Eric Ouellette, was suspended from his job for a little while. He had traded some of his work time with other firefighters so that he could be on the show. This was against the rules of his fire company.

## Counseling for Reality TV

The stress of being on a reality show is strong, so TV producers are careful about whom they choose. They want people who are healthy in both their minds and their bodies. Everybody therefore has to have strict testing before they are accepted.

Many producers also offer to send people to counseling if they have mental health problems after being on a show. At least one group of therapists focuses just on people who are having emotional problems after appearances on reality TV. This is a growing field. These therapists have already counseled hundreds of clients!

Sometimes the trouble is more serious. For example, Richard Hatch, the first *Survivor* winner, cheated on his income taxes. He won $1 million on the show and made more afterward because of his fame. But he did not pay taxes on this money, so he went to jail.

And Jennifer Crisafulli, known as Jennifer C. on *The Apprentice*, got a double whammy of bad

In this court sketch, a judge tells *Survivor* winner Richard Hatch the penalty for not paying taxes.

luck. First she was kicked off the show. ("You're fired!") Then she lost her real job. The reason was that she had said something on TV that was anti-Semitic.

# Back to "Normal" Life

Many others have said that it was hard for them to go back to their normal lives. They say that they were angry, depressed, and afraid for months after being on reality TV. This seems especially true for people who were kicked off their shows early, not for finalists.

For example, Katie Gold was voted off the Australian version of *Survivor*. While it was being filmed, she says, the producers made her into "the bad guy." Katie came close to a mental breakdown

## From Bad to Good

Bad things sometimes happen on reality TV. But some contestants turn bad into good. *Survivor* contestant Mike Skupin fell into the tribe's campfire. He was severely burned. But he recovered fully. Now he is a public speaker. He tries to inspire people. People know Skupin as the guy who fell into the fire. His Web site even has a logo of a man surrounded by flames!

Contestants on *Survivor: Cook Islands* work together to get ahead in the game.

while the show was being filmed. She says now that life afterwards has been very difficult. Even just walking down the street can trigger waves of fear and anger in her.

Janu Tornell, who quit *Survivor: Palau*, had a similar experience. She was so upset that she hid in her house for a month. And Lynn Warren, who was kicked off *The Amazing Race*, also had trouble afterward. She says that life afterward was hard because it seemed so dull: "You come back and you're really excited, and you have to go back to your regular life that you've left for two months. We would do so

Teammates on *The Amazing Race* wait for their next clue in Vietnam.

much in 12 hours on the race. Then, you come home and sit around for 12 hours. In 12 hours on the race, you've already visited three countries."[14]

# More Serious Problems

A few people on reality shows have experienced much more serious problems. For example, a winner on the Portuguese *Big Brother* quickly spent all his money and no longer felt popular. He became depressed and threatened to kill himself.

That man got help, but at least one person did not do as well. In 1997 Sinisa Savija was on *Expedition: Robinson*, the Swedish show that inspired *Survivor*. However, he was voted off the show's Southeast Asian island.

A month later, back in Sweden, Sinisa killed himself. He was worried that the show's producers

## Real Tragedy

New York firefighter Angel Juarbe won $250,000 in 2001. This was the top prize on a show called *Murder in Small Town X*. Juarbe beat nine other contestants. They were trying to track down a fictional killer. Juarbe did not get to enjoy his victory for long. He died one week later in the 9/11 terrorist attack in New York City.

would edit the show to make him look bad. His widow said, "He was a glad and stable person before he went away, and when he came back he told me, 'They are going to cut away the good things I did and make me look like a fool, to show that I was the worst and that I was the one that had to go.'"[15]

Luckily, these are not typical. Most people on reality shows have a good time—as do the viewers who follow them every week. For them, reality TV is fun and entertaining. Sometimes it even teaches them something, or it is inspiring. For these reasons, reality TV will surely be here for a long time to come.

# Notes

## Introduction: Reality TV Invades Earth!

1. Pam Sitt, "Braving Rain, 9,000 Try to Shine at 'American Idol' Audition," *Seattle Times,* September 20, 2006.

## Chapter 1: What Is Reality TV?

2. Quoted in Paula Bok, "From Reality TV to Real Life." *Seattle Times* (*Pacific Northwest* magazine), September 10, 2006, p. 27.

## Chapter 2: How Real Is Reality TV?

3. Quoted in Doug Elfman, "Naughty Secrets of Reality TV," *Chicago Sun-Times,* October 26, 2005.

4. Quoted in "In the Nick of Time," *Malay Mail,* September 21, 2006.

5. Quoted in Liz Fox, "Unreal TV: Taking a Chance on Stardom," Columbia News Ser-

vice, March 14, 2004. www.jrn.columbia.edu/studentwork/cns/2004-03-15/528.asp.

6. James Poniewozik, "How Reality TV Fakes It," *Time,* January 29, 2006. http://strweb1 12. websys.aol.com/time/magazine/article/ 0, 9171,1154194,00.html.

# Chapter 3: Reality TV Goes Global

7. Quoted in Marcela Sanchez, "Fighting Gangs with Reality TV," *Washington Post,* February 23, 2006.

8. Quoted in Edward Wong, "In War's Chaos, Iraq Finds Inspiration for Reality TV," *New York Times,* August 28, 2005.

9. Quoted in Simon Robinson, "Reality TV, African Style," *Time,* June 23, 2003.

10. Quoted in Robinson, "Reality TV, African Style."

# Chapter 4: Real Life After Reality TV

11. Quoted in Jesamyn Go, "He's a Loser, Baby, but William Hung, 'American Idol' Reject, Found Fame Anyway," MSNBC, February 26, 2004. www.msnbc.msn.com/id/4305972/.

12. Quoted in Go, "He's a Loser, Baby, but William Hung, 'American Idol' Reject, Found Fame Anyway."

13. Quoted in Luke Benedictus, "Big Bother." *The Age* (Australia), April 27, 2003.

14. Quoted in Derrik J. Lang, "Experiencing Life After Reality TV 'Death,'" Associated Press, May 25, 2005.

15. Quoted in Luke Benedictus, "Big Bother."

# Glossary

**anti-Semitic:** Prejudiced against Jewish people.

**competition:** Contests between two or more people.

**contestant:** Someone who participates in a contest.

**dialogue:** Words spoken by someone on a show.

**frankenbiting:** Putting different parts of a TV show's sound and video together.

**historical:** Having to do with history.

**hoax:** a fake.

**sitcoms:** Short for "situation comedies," the usual form of comedies on TV.

# Bibliography

## Books

Matthew Robinson, *How to Get on Reality TV.* New York: Random House Reference, 2005. This is an easy-to-read advice book, with useful interviews of insiders.

John Saade and Joe Borgenicht, *The Reality TV Handbook.* Philadelphia: Quirk, 2004. Another how-to guide, this book features a foreword by Evan Marriott, "Joe Millionaire" himself.

## Newspaper and Magazine Articles

Paula Bok, "From Reality TV to Real Life," *Seattle Times* (*Pacific Northwest* magazine), September 10, 2006. An interesting profile of a finalist on *The Biggest Loser.*

Doug Elfman, "Naughty Secrets of Reality TV," *Chicago Sun-Times,* October 26, 2005. This article tells all about how reality TV can trick viewers.

James Poniewozik, "How Reality TV Fakes It," *Time,* January 29, 2006. A detailed look at the tricks reality TV can play.

James Poniewozik, "Why Reality TV Is Good for Us," *Time,* February 17, 2003. An argument, by the magazine's TV critic, on why those who dislike reality TV are mistaken.

# Web Sites

**Reality Blurred.** www.realityblurred.com/reality tv/. A reality TV news and analysis site.

**Reality TV World.** www.realitytvworld.com/. This site features news and information about a wide range of shows.

**Tvgasm.** www.tvgasm.com/. This is a gossipy site for news, rumors, and information.

# Index

tricks by, 19–20, 24,
  26–27, 29–30
see also editing
Project Runway (TV series),
  22
Punk'd (TV series), 29

Queer Eye (TV series), 13, 14
Quest (TV series), 34–35

reality TV
  effects of, 7, 39–53
  history of, 6, 9
  popularity of, 4–6, 11,
    13–14, 18, 30
  real life compared to, 7–8,
    13, 18–30, 51–52
Real World, The (TV series),
  15, 21–22, 31
Restaurant, The (TV series),
  26
Richie, Nicole (star), 17

Saturday Night Live (TV series), 43
Savija, Sinisa (contestant),
  52–53
Sebik, Justin (contestant), 45
secrets, 16, 22
Ship, The (TV series), 25
Simple Life, The (TV series),
  17–18, 24
Simpson, Jessica (star), 23
sitcoms, 57
Skupin, Mike (contestant),
  49

sound bites, 20
Stillman, Stacey (contestant),
  26–27
story lines, 7, 19, 24, 26, 30,
  49
stress, 43, 47–53
stunt shows, 9, 34
Survivor (TV series), 4, 11,
  26–27, 33, 48–51
Sweden, 33, 52–53

Takeshi's Castle (TV series),
  34
Texas Ranch House (TV se-
  ries), 15, 18
therapists, 47
Tornell, Janu (contestant),
  50–51
Trading Spaces (TV series),
  12, 33
Trick My Truck (TV series),
  12
tricks, 19–20, 24, 26–27,
  29–30
Trump, Donald (star), 11
Truth or Consequences (TV series), 9

Uang Kaget (Surprise Money,
  TV series), 34
United States, 33

Warren, Lynn (contestant),
  51–52
women, in Arab Countries,
  33

# Picture Credits

Cover: © Getty Images

AP Photo/Charles Krupa, 14
AP Photo/Charlie Hall, 48
AP Photo/Damian Dovarganes, 27
AP Photo/East Valley Tribune, Heidi Huber, 36
AP Photo/Kevork Djansezian, 5
AP Photo/Jennifer Graylock, 27
AP Photo/Katy Pinnock, 39
AP Photo/MTV, 32
AP Photo/Mark J. Terrill, 16
Bill Inoshita/CBS/Landov, 50
Bloomberg News/Landov, 17
CBS/Landov, 6, 9, 10
Chris Pizzello/Reuters/Landov, 12
David Rae Morris/Reuters/Landov, 44
Jupiterimages Unlimited/Nonstock, 20
Jupiterimages Unlimited/Radius, 8
Jupiterimages Unlimited/Workbook, 21
Matt Kent/Photoshot/Landov, 35
Maury Aaseng, 25, 28
Reuters/Fred Prouser/Landov, 26
Reuters/Landov, 38, 40, 42
Robert Galbraith/Reuters/Landov, 46
Robert Voets/CBS/Landov, 51
WENN/Landov, 23

# About the Author

Adam Woog has written many books for adults, young adults, and children. He lives in Seattle, Washington, with his wife Karen and their daughter Leah.